BILL GATES:

Austin Brooks

BILL GATES:
COMPETITION STRATEGIES
FROM THE MASTER

Learn the competition strategies used by Bill Gates and
how to apply his competitive methods to succeed in
your life

© 2016 by Austin Brooks
© 2016 by UNIBOOKS
All rights reserved

Published by UNIBOOKS

TABLE OF CONTENTS

1. COMPETING FROM DAY ONE

1.1 Not All Fun and Games: Friendly Competition in Family and Play

1.2 A Promising Start: Middle School Successes

1.3 Prizes and Penalties

1.4 So You Weren't Born a Gates? How to Apply These Strategies to Your Life

2. BEYOND SUCCESS IN THE CLASSROOM

2.1 Traf-O-Data: MoneyMaking Contributions to Society at 17

2.2 Harvard Experience

2.3 Beyond Classroom Success: How to Apply this Strategy to Your Life

3. MAKING MICROSOFT: THE BEGINNINGS OF A COMPETITIVE COMPANY

3.1 BASIC Beginnings

3.2 Competition in the Workplace: Forming a Productive Company

3.3 Collaboration with IBM

3.4 How to Apply this Strategy in your Life

4. NO SURVIVORS: GATES AND HIS COMPETITORS

4.1 Strategies and Tactics

4.2 Dealing with Big Brother

4.3 Unlikely Friends: Microsoft and Apple

5. COLLABORATIVE AND COMBATIVE: GATES AS MANAGER

5.1 Company Roles

5.2 Abrasive yet Effective

5.3 Transition from Leadership

5.4 How to Apply This Strategy in Your Life

6. THE CASE FOR COMPETITION AS A FORCE FOR POSITIVE CHANGE

6.1 The Bill and Melinda Gates Foundation

6.2 Introducing Competition and Philanthropy

6.3 The Reinvent the Toilet Challenge: Initiatives for Productive Change

6.4 Competition for Good: How to Apply this Strategy to Your Life

7 COMPETITIVE SUCCESS: NOT WITHOUT CRITICISM

7.1 Antitrust Case

7.2 Peer Accounts

7.3 Personal Life and Responses to Criticism

7.4 How to Approach Criticisms of the Competition in Your Life

1. COMPETING FROM DAY ONE

Bill Gates was born with undeniable intellectual talent: his feats of memorization and intelligence even from a young age are impressive.

But there was an aspect of his life that he wasn't born with and that needed to be fostered: an atmosphere of competition that surrounded him from day one. A consciousness of healthy competition began as early as Gates' family life, where his parents implemented well-defined rewards for successes and penalties for failures. Every phase of his formative years was molded by this integration of competition into all his pursuits, from sports to schoolwork.

1.1 Not All Fun and Games: Competition in Family and Play

Born William Henry Gates III, the child who was to become the richest man in the world drew his first breath on October 28, 1955 in Seattle, Washington. He became part of an upper-middle class family that was well-educated and carried a prestigious background: his father, William H. Gates Sr., was a successful lawyer, and his mother, a former schoolteacher, held a seat on the boards of various organizations, including United Way and IBM.

Along with older sister Kristianne and younger sister Libby, all three of the Gates children were encouraged to involve competition into many aspects of their lives, from serious undertakings like academics to more frivolous pastimes like childhood playtime. He took on leadership roles even in the most casual of circumstances: At the family summer house on Puget Sound, Gates took responsibility for coordinating family athletic games. In addition, he loved board games, dominating in Monopoly.

Many of Gates' pursuits as a young child arose not only out of a desire to compete with others, but also clearly demonstrated a thirst for knowledge and intellectual stimulation. He devoured books and easily conquered the entire World Book Encyclopedia set by age 8. He baffled his Sunday School confirmation class when, challenged to memorize chapters 5-7 of the Book of Matthew, he delivered the 2,000-word passage flawlessly.

This combination of a natural aptitude for intellectual pursuits and a pure hunger for intellectual challenge and stimulation set Gates up to excel from a young age. Nonetheless, his childhood was not a smooth one.

His family life exposed him to a high-achieving, competitive environment from the very beginning, simply by observing his parents. He had a close, albeit volatile, relationship with his mother. Thanks to her role in civic charities and various corporate boards, Gates was often invited to accompany her to various volunteer opportunities and meetings of community organizations.

He tended towards being a problematic child: neither a people-pleaser nor a rule-follower, he only gained satisfaction from getting his way. Sometimes described as an argumentative nuisance, Gates was never satisfied with settling for a loss, even over trivial issues among his family. Regardless of whether the argument was with his mother about cleaning his room or with his father about sitting still at the dinner table, he insisted on getting his way and made his family dinners frequently unpleasant and impossible.

Luckily for Gates, his parents chose not to stifle his eccentricities, and instead found ways to channel his abilities towards productive means. Consuming knowledge at a stunning pace and, despite behavioral concerns, showing intellectual capacity far beyond his age, his parents employed the 11-year-old as a greeter at their social gatherings and put him to work at his father's professional events. At 11 years old, Gates was already being treated as an adult.

Still concerned about his behavior, his parents sought outside help. A therapist suggested that they loosen up, and instead give their son a degree of relative independence. They loosened the reins and found ways to give Gates the freedom to pursue individual projects and make more decisions in his young life.

Since he no longer had to compete with his parents for freedom, Gates began to find competitors in the outside world and, beyond that, began to find success.

1.2 A Promising Start: Middle School Successes

A turning point in Gates' education came in 1967 when his parents enrolled him in one of Seattle's exclusive prep schools. Despite a deep-rooted respect for public education, Gates' parents were committed to finding a way to challenge their son's intellectual abilities, and Lakeside School turned out the be exactly what he needed.

The attitude that Gates took towards technology and the newly presented opportunities were critical in what was to come. When the Mother's Club at the school used the proceeds from his school's rummage sale to buy a teletype and computer time for Lakeside students, he jumped at the opportunity to cash in on his talents. He took full advantage of this program to develop his skills and ended up developing his first computer game: a version of tic-tac-toe in which the user was able to play against the computer.

Eventually, the school ran out of the money necessary for purchasing computer time. Not one to follow the rules when an opportunity was on the line, Gates hacked into the computer and found a way to use it for free. Gates didn't achieve his early successes by pleasing his superiors and following set paths of behavior. Even as a teenager, he was constantly pushing limits and getting outside the comfortable boundaries of expectations for his age group.

1.3 Prizes and Penalties

In 1970, at age 15, Gates partnered up with his friend Paul Allen, and the two began a quest to create innovative solutions to local problems using computers, a quest that would last decades, although Gates himself might not have guessed so. With Allen's help, the two created a payroll program for Information Sciences, Inc. and a system to measure traffic data and earned $20,000 from their second venture. Their early success was riddled with challenges and obstacles, but, especially for Gates, the greatest of all of these was losing.

This mindset had been inscribed on Gates from a young age. According to a visitor to the family's home, "It didn't matter whether it was Hearts or pickle ball or swimming to the dock...there was always a reward for winning and there was always a penalty for losing." This applied as much to the playful games of childhood as it did to the serious money-making and problem-solving pursuits of Gates' teenage years.

1.4 So You Weren't Born a Gates? How to Apply These Strategies to Your Life

It is without doubt that Gates was born with incredible intellectual talent. He scored 1590 out of 1600 on his SAT's and memorized a 2,000 word passage at the age of 11. Regardless of your natural talent, however, there are certain takeaways from Gates' life story that you can pull from on your search for success.

From Monopoly to his middle school company, Gates was constantly pushing himself and those around him to be better and to stay ahead of everyone else. But as a child, he wasn't coordinating family game schedules and creating tic-tac-toe programs for monetary gain; he genuinely loved what he was doing and felt driven to continue to his search for minute possibilities for solutions to problems and improvements to what he was doing every day.

In your own search for success, monetarily or otherwise, consider the following questions:

-How can you find joy and competition in everyday tasks?

-How can you make each task or project you are working on a little bit better?

-What are some ways you could use your own talents to get a step ahead your nearest competitors?

Even by asking yourself these questions, you are cultivating within yourself an awareness of the competitive environment surrounding you. Only once you are aware of these factors can you succeed. Gates was well aware of the challenges facing him as a child and adolescent: his parents' rules, his school administrators, local law. He fought constantly against them.

The second takeaway from the formative years of Gates' childhood is the importance of finding collaborators. Almost from the beginning, Gates wouldn't have achieved what he did if it weren't for his partner in success. As we will see in later chapters, Allen was not solely an encouraging friend who supported all of Gates' ideas; the two would have strong disagreements and explosive arguments.

Even if it's just a friend or a coworker to bounce ideas off of over coffee, never underestimate the power of collaboration when it comes to achieving your goals. To get one step ahead of the rest, you need the feedback and input of a teammate.

Just like Gates excelled through partnering with Paul Allen, find someone who shares a common enthusiasm and who pushes you to succeed. Are you looking for success in your personal training business? Align yourself with a talented trainer and accept their criticism and feedback. Are you a writer? Actively seek out writing groups or peers to edit your work, people who provide you with the kind of collaborative, competitive partnerships that started Gates on the path to billionaire status.

2. BEYOND SUCCESS IN THE CLASSROOM

On numerous occasions during his adolescence and early 20's, Gates managed to turn around a number of events that could have been labeled failures. He took full advantage of his education by pushing beyond the boundaries of the classroom and refusing to follow the traditional expectations of what high school and college excellence meant. Throughout his many years of education, Gates' intelligence was only a single factor in his repeated successes. His competitive spirit and desire to succeed drove him to excel in various innovative entrepreneurial efforts. This chapter takes us deeper into Gates' main projects before starting Microsoft and allows us to examine the main aspects of his early years that contributed to his later success.

2.1 Traf-O-Data: Money Making Contributions to Society at 17

Not content with the traditional methods for recording traffic data, Gates and his partner Allen used the needs of the community as the perfect opening for a moneymaking opportunity. Let's be clear: this was not an altruistic venture that was solely meant to help the community become more efficient. The two young entrepreneurs recognized that they could create products that were helpful and, more importantly, profitable.

Traf-O-Data, their name for this particular business, was formed with the goal of computerizing traffic data to create reports for county law enforcement. When they began, the two became competitive not on their own accord: they had to make use of the resources available to them. Classmates helped them the read the hole-patterns on the paper tape (recorded when cars passed by a certain point on a road) and transcribe them for the computer, which then allowed Gates and Allen to produce the reports.

Through various mutual friends, they recruited Paul Gilbert to help them create the hardware to read the hole-patterns automatically, as they lacked the skills to build the actual machine. However, when they tried to sell their service to the local county, the machine didn't work on the first demo. Says Gates of the experience, "It didn't work. We ended up being ok successful, not seriously successful…just by processing the tapes. At first that was a very manual process. Then we used this prototype machine that we built to do that. So, we made a little bit of money and had some fun with it."

The venture ultimately came to an end when Washington state offered free traffic processing services, and the county no longer needed Traf-O-Data's product. In May 1979, the hopeful project was suspended for good. But, as it turns out, the duo's ultimate failure in measuring traffic patterns could have contributed to the ultimate success of their next great venture: Microsoft. As we will discuss later in the chapter, the way that Gates and Allen used the lessons from this failure provided them with the tools for later success.

2.2 Harvard Experience

After scoring an impressive 1590 out of 1600 on the SAT (and sharing his score with anyone who would listen), Gates entered Harvard University in 1973. This elite college offered an atmosphere of competitive surroundings with the kinds of challenge that would allow Gates to thrive. He stayed in touch with Allen, and continued to make connections that would help him in the future. However, he clearly continued to forge his own path. "I decided that I would be different and never attend any class I was signed up for, but always attend a class I wasn't signed for", said Gates recently in an Ask Me Anything on Reddit.

2.3 Beyond Classroom Success: How to Apply this Strategy to Your Life

This period of Gates' life provides you with three critical takeaways regarding competition: creating success from failure, jumping at timely opportunities, and surrounding yourself with a competitive environment in order to succeed.

First, look back at your own recent failures and consider them in the light of the following questions:

- What were the elements of success, even if the project as a whole did not reach the desired goal?
- Why did the project fail?
- What would you change if you had an opportunity to try again?

Let's take our writer example from the last chapter. What if you are a writer and you wrote an article that was not well received by your desired audience? As much as you might want to bury that experience in the back of your mind and forget it forever, taking advantage of the opportunity to reflect on the reasons for failure will serve you more than forgetting it ever will.

Write down your reflections right now, while the failure is still fresh. If you file away failures without taking the opportunity to draw valuable feedback from them, you will never move forward because you will continue to make the same mistakes. This reflection on failure doesn't have to be entirely positive: remember that drive to achieve your objective. For some, frustration at failure can be a source of motivation towards success in the future. Gates and Allen were so driven to develop a working machine during their Traf-O-Data project that their failure only provided them with greater impetus towards their goals.

Allen summed it up well when he said, "Traf-O-Data remains my favorite mistake because it confirmed to me that every failure contains the seeds of your next success." To be a competitor in a market saturated with close contenders, you must have knowledge of potential mistakes. For Gates and Allen, their Traf-O-Data experience was an opportunity to test ideas and gain experience so that they could be competitive when it really mattered.

Secondly, you should take away that time is crucial. If you are chasing your dreams, it is of primary importance to have a plan. Awareness of the timeliness of your opportunities could make or break your venture. Maybe you aren't planning to radically change the world (or maybe you are); either way, you need to be aware of moments when, if you don't take the opportunity to make your project a success, someone else will. Gates could have waited two years and followed the traditional path of graduating college before embarking on a business venture. But he sensed that this was the critical moment to make his dream of what was to be Microsoft a reality, and he is now the richest man in the world.

And for the final lesson of Gates' pre-Microsoft years, surround yourself with competition. If you don't have a competitive environment, you will not be pushed to succeed. It is debatable whether Gates was truly challenged at Harvard, judging by his recent admission of not attending any of the classes he was enrolled in. Ultimately, however, he took it upon himself to leave two years into his college career in pursuit of his dreams and in search of a competitive environment that would later secure his entrepreneurial success.

Armod with the knowledge of failure, the perfect opportunity, and an environment of healthy competition, Bill Gates was ready to leave Harvard and take on the real world.

3. MAKING MICROSOFT: THE BEGINNINGS OF A COMPETITIVE COMPANY

It all began when Gates got his hands on an article in *Popular Electronics*, an article that featured the Altair 8800 mini-computer kit. It was the first personal computer in the world, and Gates and Allen were both ignited with a passion and an enthusiasm that envisioned the future possibilities around personal computing. They were further ignited with the fire of competition: they had to work fast to stay ahead of the competition in the newly launched race to develop software for the personal computer.

This chapter follows the development of Microsoft as a collaborative endeavor, one that was constantly driven by the competition between Microsoft and its closest rivals.

3.1 BASIC Beginnings

Altair was manufactured by a company called Micro Instrumentation and Technology Systems (MITS). Using their sense of timing and opportunity, Gates and Allen jumped on this opportunity to become real players in the computer industry.

They knew that they were racing against time; they couldn't wait for a thoroughly tested, working demo. They contacted MITS, claiming that they had a BASIC software program that would run on the company's Altair computer.

Of course, they didn't actually have the program ready; rather, they wanted to gauge the interest of the company about their potential product. When the president of MITS requested a demo, they used a combination of total dedication, resourcefulness, and luck to produce a program that actually ran on the Altair computer. When Allen was hired by MITS as a result of the program's promising success, Gates left Harvard soon after to join him in a partnership that would change the world.

3.2 Competition in the Workplace: Forming a Productive Company

Upon the birth of their partnership in 1975, the two young entrepreneurs chose the name Micro-soft, blending the idea of a microcomputer and software together. Despite the miraculous early success, it wasn't initially earning a profit because of computer enthusiasts' ability to copy and distribute software amongst themselves. Gates learned a startling figure about the product that he had invested so much time in: only about 10 percent of the users of his software actually paid for it.

Always on the cutting edge of industry, Gates had a unique view: making people pay for software contributed to greater production and improved innovation, while allowing free distribution discouraged developers from innovative products, since there was no monetary incentive.

His view basically guaranteed greater competition in the industry, because other developers would be more motivated to produce new quality products. Gates *wanted* more competition. He wanted to be challenged, and he wanted to challenge others. He understood that money was more than a selfish desire for wealth, but rather it was a way to motivate creativity of invention.

Microsoft's rise was not without conflict. Gates and Roberts, the MITS president, clashed frequently, and in 1977, Roberts separated from Gates and Allen, leaving his company in the hands of a new owner. Gates and Allen sued for the rights to their software.

In 1979, the company moved to Seattle. They had 25 employees, and had earned a total of $2.5 million that year. At the age of 23, Gates was marked for success.

Let's focus on two key contributing factors to the company's ascent. First, Gates fiercely defended his creation and was adamant in making sure everything produced by his company was absolutely the best it could be. He is even known for correcting code himself. Some might call this obsessive, but it can be said without a doubt that Gate's obsession for perfection left nothing up to chance.

Second, let's consider his fearlessness. He wasn't intimidated by competition, but rather saw competitors as opponents that needed to be defeated on his way to the top. Neither his age nor his inexperience were factors when he considered whether he could stand up to a difficult task. In Chapter 5, we will dive further into Gates' management style and his interactions within the company, but for now, consider his fearless attitude towards external competitors.

Slowly, the competition began to grow, and Microsoft was no longer alone in the world of choices for computing software. Gates' ability to compete with others and prioritize the growth and development of his company kept Microsoft well ahead of the rest.

3.3 Collaboration with IBM

IBM approached Gates in 1980: they wanted him to develop a BASIC interpreter to run on their machine, a personal computer (PC). Always an opportunist, when IBM requested to purchase the source code from Gates, he refused, but sold them only the license, so that he would continue to earn money for each copy sold with their computers, which turned out to be a significant quantity.

For Gates, the key takeaway from this partnership was the importance of collaboration. Despite the fact that IBM was one of his biggest competitors, he took advantage of an opportunity to collaborate with them, to their mutual advantage. He used strategic methods to ensure that success was always on his side. This was never more evident than in the case of Gates' experience with IBM.

Although IBM produced the hardware of the machine, the world quickly realized that Gates held the magic behind the PC, and his company exploded. They grew from 25 employees to 128 in two years, and revenue grew from $2.5 million to over $16 million in two years.

3.4 How to Apply this Strategy in your Life

This era of Gates' life was critical to his success. Let's focus on three key takeaways from those years of rapid ascent that were fundamental in leading to billionaire status:

- Use money as a positive, healthy motivator
- Identify your competitors
- Always keep the ball in your court

First, Gates found a way to use money as a healthy motivator. He didn't allow it to turn him into a money-hungry monster by losing sight of long-term goals in favor of instant gratification. But at the same time, he also didn't turn into a self-sacrificing giver to all. Look back at the open letter he wrote to the community of those who pursued computers as a hobby. Regardless of how unpopular the idea was at the time, he argued that the free distribution of software was damaging innovation in the industry as a whole. He recognized the value that money has in encouraging competition, and the underlying need for competition to inspire innovation.

Keep this lesson present in your personal and entrepreneurial pursuits. Some tend to demonize money as an evil, deceptive goal. However, if you can strike a healthy balance between money as a source of inspiration and innovation (but not the only source), it can be one of your biggest tools.

Second, it is imperative that you identify your competitors. From early on in the company's history, Gates new that Apple, Intel, and IBM were the biggest threats to his company's growth. He ceaselessly traveled to spread knowledge of the benefits of Microsoft's applications to stay ahead during his competitors' rise. Then, when he had the opportunity, he strategically partnered with IBM to cement Microsoft's rise.

Who are your biggest competitors? Who are those who threaten to overtake your success? Whether those competitors are personal or professional, identify their advantages over you and make yourself aware of what you can do to cement your lead.

Finally, always keep the ball in your court. Once you have identified your competitors and considered the role of money in your ventures, use this consciousness to find ways to keep the advantage. In Gates' case, he refused to sell the source code used in IBM's PCs, which allowed him to charge for each copy sold with the machine, which ultimately earned him millions of dollars and paved for the way for even greater success in the future.

4. NO SURVIVORS: GATES AND HIS COMPETITORS

Bill Gate's competitive drive has been discussed and alluded to throughout this book as a trait that allowed him to be so successful. This drive propelled him into dominance in the field of software. This chapter will explore his relationship with his competitors by going into more detail about his business practices. This competitive behavior will then be analyzed within the context of the antitrust lawsuit filed by the U.S. government against Microsoft and, on a more personal level, Bill Gate's competition with the leader of Apple, Steve Jobs.

4.1 Strategies and Tactics

The methods used by Bill Gates to create his business empire have often been criticized on ethical, even legal, grounds; however, the one area in which they cannot be criticized is their efficacy.

Like all companies, Microsoft started small: it was at the mercy of the bigger players and susceptible to the same practices Gates would later user on smaller companies. However, Microsoft was in an industry that was relatively undeveloped and just coming into its own. Obviously, companies like Google, Yahoo, Amazon, or even Apple and HP did not possess anything near their current importance at that time. IBM was the giant of the industry at the time of

Microsoft's beginnings, and Gates ended up collaborating with them for a time. Traversing the business waters at the helm of a small company is not an easy task, yet Bill Gates did so in an astoundingly successful way. How?

As discussed in the first chapter, Gates was an all-star student, a competitive entrepreneur, and a businessman with a keen sense of timing. In developing his company, he used all three traits to gain an advantage. Gates not only understand the technology on which his company was formed, but, more importantly, he understood the market. This proved to be a deadly combination when it came to his competitors.

One strategy Microsoft employed was "embrace, extend, and extinguish". This three step process allowed Microsoft to gain a foothold in different markets, expand that foothold, and throw all competitors off their perches. Here's how it worked: Microsoft develops a product that works well and is compatible with the product of a competing company; Microsoft then "extends" that product by adding or promoting new features that are unique and incompatible with their competitors product; over time, Microsoft's new product with the additional features corners the market by pushing out the original competitors. This is highly aggressive and intelligent: by identifying a market where room for growth exists, Gates was able to fully develop the potential of Microsoft.

Along with this strategy, the use of litigation goes hand in hand: protecting the exclusive copyrights Microsoft has over the functions that make their product superior. When a competitor saw the advantages that Microsoft's product had, they would occasionally attempt to produce something similar. By using legal means, Gates prevented his competitors from infringing on the copyrights to disrupt Microsoft's dominance.

Market share was vital to Microsoft's success. And in order to gain more and more, products were entered into markets at prices lower than that of their competitors, naturally earning the preference of consumer. Or, instead of lower prices, products would occasionally be given away to encourage consumers to purchase other Microsoft software. This created an environment where Microsoft became the natural choice: if you already had Microsoft software that worked great, when it came time to buy something else, why wouldn't you chose Microsoft? By giving people a taste, Gates ensured that they would come back for more.

The final practice in Gate's business armory was the control of information. Microsoft was not an open book and not everyone who was interested in it was given equal access. For example, when releasing new software or giving a big announcement, reporters who enjoyed the trust of the company were given greater access. Gates knew how important perception was and did not want the chance to influence it to be haphazardly given away. Therefore, he

31

carefully controlled how the public received information from and about Microsoft.

4.2 Dealing with Big Brother

Some of these practices ultimately came back to bite Microsoft. On May 18, 1998 the U.S. Department of Justice, with the further backing of 20 states, filed an antitrust lawsuit against Microsoft. The case would last more than two years before a verdict was finally reached.

The case was a complicated one and still is open to much interpretation. The basic argument of the prosecution was that Microsoft used its position as a monopoly to prevent competition. One of the largest issues at hand was the coupling of Internet Explorer with Microsoft Windows. Microsoft realized the importance of the Internet before it became the dominant global force of today, and it wanted to grab and hold onto all the Internet users it could, so it made Internet Explorer a key element of Microsoft Windows. The prosecution argued that this was an unfair use of its power and that the two should be separate, allowing users to choose what Internet Browser they wanted.

Much of the debate about Internet Browsers was focused on Netscape, an early competitor in this field. Netscape is interesting because it represents one of those moments in Gates' life when he found himself at a disadvantage. Netscape in fact beat Microsoft into the Internet Browser market. They forced Microsoft to play catch-up, which they did in almost no time. Entering an uneven playing field where Netscape had a 90% market share before Microsoft had a product, Gates pushed his company to develop a competitor, Internet Explorer, and then used his business acumen to promote it and get consumers to use it more than they used Netscape. By 2000, the tables had turned: Internet Explorer now had 95% of the market, while Netscape was barely an afterthought. The practices which Gates used to crush Netscape and ensure his product's success were later used against him in the antitrust case.

In the end, Microsoft lost the case. There was a brief period where it looked as if the company would be broken into two separate units, but this penalty was never applied. Microsoft offered to change a number of its practices and paid fines, which the government accepted.

Gates' most visible role in all this was a deposition he gave. He was asked a number of questions by the prosecuting attorney and was almost comically roundabout in answering them. Gates would debate the most simple of words with the attorney and refused to fall into the traps set to make him admit to anti-competitive practices. In fact, Gates was so evasive in answering the questions that the judge laughed while watching a tape of the deposition. Microsoft's own attorneys were worried that the tape might hurt public perception of Gates, so they did their best to paint the tape as unrepresentative of the deposition as a whole and the norm for such things.

Despite the ruling against them, Microsoft remained a juggernaut in the technology field and continued to set the bar for excellence. As for Gates, there has been speculation that the lawsuit helped him along in his decision to leave Microsoft. Having built one of the most influential and powerful companies in the history of the world, Gates was content to step aside and let someone follow in his footsteps.

4.3 Unlikely Friends: Microsoft and Apple

Microsoft and Apple stand large in both the history and the present of the personal computer industry, and they are also largely seen as the product of two individuals: Bill Gates and Steve Jobs. They were competitors even since the two companies began, but the nature of the competition has swung back and forth between adversarial and amicable. Gates himself said it best when summed up their relationship this way: we grew up together.

The relationship began as early as the late 1970s when Gates and his outfit worked with Apple and wrote software for some of the very first Macs. Much of Microsoft's early work was done on the Mac, and Gates even went so far as to say that, "We had more people working on the Mac than [Jobs] did". The two companies worked closely together until Gates' ambition outgrew the role that he played in Apple, and he chose to develop software for IBM as well, rather than just for Apple. Jobs was furious and felt that Gates was using all the work they had done collaboratively for his own profit.

The relationship was to continue in a similar vein throughout the remainder of the 80s and for a good part of the 90s. Microsoft and Apple were direct competitors for the same market, offering products that were similar, yet fundamentally different. While Jobs and Apple in general prided themselves on design and look, Gates was more interested in pushing functionality. While Apple was struggling to grow, Microsoft was surging ahead and dominating the market, in large part due to the efforts and strategies of Gates.

As both men grew older, things between them became friendlier, especially when Steve Jobs was diagnosed with the illness that was to end his life. Gates and Jobs appeared together publically on a number of occasions in the past decade or so and often lauded the other, even going so far as to say they were friends. However, certain comments made by both revealed that a degree of competition remained between the two. For example, Gates dismissed Apple's products as something he never wished his company had created.

For two men who were so passionately involved in the day-to-day running of their respective companies and sought to always win, they developed a deep degree of respect for one another. The competition between Gates and Jobs and their respective companies pushed both to succeed, but stayed within the limits of healthy competition, encouraging innovation and not souring towards unproductive ugliness.

5. COLLABORATIVE AND COMBATIVE: GATES AS MANAGER

Gates had the reputation of being distant, combative, and critical of his company's managers while he acted as the chief executive. This chapter examines the role of competition in his leadership positions at Microsoft, and allows us to pick and choose the aspects of his competitive leadership that can serve you, and those that should be avoided.

5.1 Company Roles

Throughout his time at Microsoft, Gates transitioned from an ambitious, quality-obsessed 23-year old to a CEO and ultimately chairman of a 71,000-person company. The roles he held during the rise of Microsoft included CEO, chairman, chief software architect, and finally, largest individual shareholder of stock until May 2014. This section of the chapter will give a brief overview of the competitive qualities Gates considers important as a manager, which allowed the company to become what it did.

1. "Develop your people to do your job better than you." Despite his fiercely competitive mindset and ambition to be the best at all costs, Gates knew that the success of his company depended on the skills of the people he employed. As obsessive as he was about quality, he could not continue to do everyone's jobs as the company continued to grow. He had to

learn to trust his managers to be as obsessive about quality and competitiveness as he was.

2. "Hire thoughtfully and be willing to fire." When a company (or project) is as closely tied to your personal success as Microsoft is to Gates' fame, you can't afford to take hiring lightly. In an article for the Wall Street Journal, Gates argued for the hiring process to be specifically focused on the aspects of the candidate that are most important. He valued talent and his strategy involves measuring and managing what you want to improve. Instead of hiring people based on what they have done in the past, for example "must have 5 years of programming experience," he argues to define the hiring process based on the objective, for example "must be able to develop X project within 6 months." This strategy puts the focus on the company and the potential contributions of the candidate, rather than on the previous experience of the candidate.

3. "Take on projects yourself." This is critical when it comes to being an effective manager: regardless of how high up in the company you move, you must continue to take on projects and allow yourself to see things from a hands-on perspective. While Gates was primarily a manager and executive at Microsoft, he also served as the chief software architect, a position he created for himself after stepping down from CEO in 2000. A manager who only delegates tasks does not remain competitive, according to Gates.

4. "Clearly define success." In order to become competitive in your chosen field, you must have a well-defined vision of exactly what it means to be successful. Don't allow it to be a vague concept that is open to interpretation. Just like Gates' family did during low-stakes Monopoly games of his childhood, clearly define the consequences of winning or losing, and make sure that everyone is aware of them.

5.2 Abrasive yet Effective

Despite Microsoft's early success and early entry into the market, Gates was keenly aware of the many threats to his Windows operating system. He knew that he had to work tirelessly to stay ahead of the competition and to ward off threats from other platforms.

As we saw in the previous chapter about the details of the antitrust litigation, Gates was not concerned with insulting others. He was not worried about pushing the limits of politeness far beyond what was generally accepted.

In a presentation during a particularly high-pressure moment of the company's history, when Windows was racing against Netscape and Sun to develop a cross-platform, Gates is recorded as saying, "There's nothing about that slide I like!" to the presenter, and later "Why don't you just give up your options and join the Peace Corps!"

There was no question that Gates was a ruthless businessman, and he applied the same principles that he used when facing his business competitors to approach his employees. Gates' extreme focus and ambition were some of his biggest tools in maintaining clear objectives. His overall goal from the beginning was dominance in software, and he never strayed or let anyone get in the way. Even as his company grew, he never fully trusted others to oversee what he knew he was the best at. Some may call this obsessive, others may call it the secret to his success. As a manager, he didn't trust others to do his tasks until he was completely confident that they were able to.

5.3 Transition from Leadership

One of the qualities that allowed Gates to be successful at Microsoft from 1975 to 2006 was his ability to adapt, change, and be one step ahead of the rest. Consider how much the world of computing and software had changed in that 30-year span. Gates' competitors were constantly evolving throughout that time frame; therefore, he and his competitive strategy had to remain flexible to constant changes.

In 2000, Gates stepped down from the position of CEO, but remained chairman and "chief software architect" a position specifically tailored for himself. He remarked that, "My announcement is not a retirement--it's a reordering of priorities." Gates, secure in the leadership of Microsoft, had found new priorities in his philanthropic activities at the Bill and Melinda Gates foundation.

5.4 How to Apply This Strategy in Your Life

Balancing effective management and ambitious drive in the way that Gates did is not easy. Using the following questions as a guide, consider the ways in which you can balance competition and management strategies in your own endeavors:

- What is the ultimate, overarching goal?
- What are the most important qualities required to achieve this goal?
- What are the qualities you possess that are most valuable in achieving this goal?
- In what capacity can you employ others to be most effective in achieving your goal?
- In what ways can you continue to be hands-on while managing others?

As stated in previous chapters, continue to be conscious of your competition and integrate this strategy of effective, competitive management into your journey towards achieving your ultimate goals. Take into account Gates' key pieces of management advice, and adapt them in your quest for success in whatever you may do.

6.THE CASE FOR COMPETITION AS A FORCE FOR POSITIVE CHANGE

Bill Gates may have stepped down from leading Microsoft, but his competitive spirit in and out of the industry perseveres. Following the death of Steve Jobs, he refuted claims of bad blood between the two by saying "We were not at war. We made great products, and competition was always a positive thing." After leaving Microsoft, he dedicated himself to trailblazing the world of philanthropy and charity, bringing his competitive strategies to the Bill and Melinda Gates Foundation. This chapter will examine the ways in which Gates has positively channeled his competitive spirit in the post-Microsoft portion of his life in order to continue growing his wealth and contributing to society.

6.1 The Bill and Melinda Gates Foundation

After meeting Melinda French in 1987, Gates and she were married in 1994. Soon after, however, his mother died of breast cancer, which had a profound impact on him. As she had played a fundamental role in making him into the man he was, particularly with regards to her positions in civic organizations and philanthropic activities, he felt compelled to do something to honor her life and continue her legacy.

With Melinda's help, he realized that he had both a desire and an obligation to donate more of his immense wealth. He founded the William H. Gates Foundation in 1994 and made a commitment to investing in education, world health, and low-income communities. In 2000, Melinda and he combined a variety of different, family related foundations into one and made a $28 billion-dollar contribution to mark the start of the Bill and Melinda Gates foundation.

As he had always done in the past, Gates continued to heavily research his passions. Now, however, his interests had transitioned toward philanthropy. He educated himself by learning about the great philanthropists of the past, including Andrew Carnegie and John D. Rockefeller.

His last full day at Microsoft was June 7, 2008, and in February 2014, he completed the transition to the position of "technical adviser" to Microsoft, allowing him to fully involve himself in his philanthropic pursuits.

6.2 Introducing Competition and Philanthropy

When we think of charities, we don't often think of cutthroat, ruthless businessmen as being the champions of fundraising for the greater good. However, just as he had done with the other passions in his life, Gates accepted nothing less than his absolute best when it came to running his foundation.

Gates continues to be a leader in terms of the public policies he supports and the employment practices he uses.

Although he may no longer be surrounded by a world of processors and programmers, Gates applies the same passion for innovation to his foundation as he did for growing his company years ago.

In one example of innovation as an employer, he provides his employees with one year of paid leave after the birth or adoption of a child, a very uncommon practice, at least in the United States.

The foundation funds projects globally. In line with Gates' competitive character, nothing about the foundation is small "We Identify challenges that can be tackled on a global level. We work with partners that can help to affect change globally, and then scale solutions to a local level." They seek to fund projects throughout the vast areas of global health, global education, and initiatives to prevent and alleviate poverty in the US. Just as he once made it his goal to put "a computer on every desk and in every home" when starting Microsoft, Gates won't settle for small projects. He is out to change the world.

6.3 The Reinvent the Toilet Challenge: Initiatives for Productive Change

By applying the same principles he used to encourage innovation in his multi-billion-dollar company, Gates used competition as a way to induce innovation in his foundation. In 2011, the Bill and Melinda Gates Foundation launched the Reinvent the Toilet Challenge to answer the question of how to decontaminate human waste without connections to water or sewage for less than five cents per user per day. In other words, they were using a competition to solve issues of sanitation and waste disposal worldwide.

As a result of the challenge, the foundation connected participants from 29 countries and representatives from communities to adopt the innovative solutions, all of which took place at a fair in their Seattle, Washington headquarters. Among the winners were projects that proposed converting human waste into fuel, biological charcoal, and minerals.

6.4 Competition for Good: How to Apply this Strategy to Your Life

Don't settle for the safe dream. Don't limit yourself. And don't put yourself in a box. Bill Gates was a "tech guy", but he and his wife have become award-winning philanthropists and true changers of the world. They have excelled on multiple stages. After leaving Microsoft, Gates has far from given up on competition; he has simply chosen bigger competitors: poverty, HIV, water contamination, and lack of education.

Practically, strategies like Gates' Reinvent the Toilet Challenge are used every day in classroom and parenting settings. Do you ever remember teachers or parents making a game out of cleaning up? Or awarding prizes to those who picked up the most trash? Gates simply took the inspiring game setting and applied it on a global, world-revolutionizing scale. Right now, think of the biggest problem or question you have. How could you turn it into a game? The next challenge is winning that game.

7. COMPETITIVE SUCCESS: NOT WITHOUT CRITICISM

When someone as large a public figure as Bill Gates has had such a high level of success, it is inevitable that criticism will be levelled against them. People have taken aim at Gates from as many different angles as they can: his business practices, his personal life, his charity work. In our final chapter, we will explore some of these criticisms and how they impact our understanding of a living legend. What can you take from Gates' experience to deal with criticisms of your own competitive endeavors?

7.1 Antitrust Case

As discussed in Chapter 4, Bill Gates and Microsoft were involved in a prominent antitrust case brought by the government, a case they eventually lost. While we've already talked about the case and some of the practices that brought it on, we didn't fully detail the criticisms.

As with all antitrust cases, the government argued that Microsoft's behavior stifled competition. How? By linking together their products, customers were almost obligated to use other Microsoft products if they already used one. If you used Microsoft Windows, you would naturally use Internet Explorer. This specific example had another twist to it. Microsoft Windows, the larger operating system, was shown to suffer slowdowns and errors when users deleted Internet Explorer off their computers; obviously encouraging people to stick with both products.

Another practice was compatibility: for a long time, Microsoft made it difficult for their smaller products, like Microsoft Office, to be run on non-Windows platforms, or they entirely held back their products from other platforms. This further encouraged people to only purchase Microsoft products since they didn't have the option of crossing software over onto different platforms.

A final facet of the criticism thrown against Gates was his practice of acquiring smaller businesses. Some of the most well-known Microsoft programs were not developed within the company, but were instead acquired through purchasing smaller software companies. For example, Microsoft PowerPoint was originally created by a company named Forethought, and was only purchased by Microsoft in 1987 for $14 million. Even such a prominent product as Internet Explorer wasn't originally designed by Microsoft, but was instead acquired from a company called SpyGlass Software.

All of these practices of Gates have been criticized for a number of reasons: limiting competition, a lack of innovation, unfair use of the company's size, even bullying. It's true that sometimes Gates' tactics were harsh and deserved criticism, it is difficult to entirely fault either he or Microsoft for doing what companies have always done. Bill Gates was a businessman, first and foremost, and he took the necessary steps to make his company succeed. Whether or not it did is clear to anyone who cares to look objectively.

7.2 Peer Accounts

In addition to the barrage of criticisms thrown at Gates during the antitrust case, many criticisms from peers and former employees have surfaced since Gates left Microsoft, calling into question his highly competitive practices.

In a critical account of Microsoft's performance review system, one former employee commented that the reviews tended to be "always much less about how I could become a better engineer and much more about my need to improve my visibility among other managers." This criticism was not unique: Gates has often been criticized in recent years for worrying about the aesthetic of Microsoft and less about innovation and development of new technologies.

Once Microsoft was already firmly established as a dominant brand, peers have said that he stopped caring as much about innovation and he cared more that products continued to align with the Microsoft aesthetic and money-making purpose. According to another senior manager, "It was top-notch, but now it's just a barren wasteland. And that's Microsoft. The company just isn't cool anymore."

In one of the most high-profile peer-accounts of Gates, Steve Jobs said in an interview

> *Bill is basically unimaginative and has never invented anything, which is why I think he's more comfortable now in philanthropy than technology. He just shamelessly ripped off other people's ideas.*

Despite the harsh criticism, Gates responded by saying

> *Over the course of the 30 years we worked together, you know, he said a lot of very nice*

49

> *things about me and he said a lot of tough*
> *things. We got to work together. We spurred*
> *each other on, even as competitors. None of*
> *that bothers me at all.*

Some attribute his polite response to the fact that he didn't want to offend Jobs after death. However, it could be that Gates was truly thankful for the competitive value of Jobs' criticism, and the way that the former Apple genius pushed him to innovate and create in ways he never could have imagined possible had he not been challenged.

7.3 Personal Life and Responses to Criticism

Among criticisms of Gates' personal life include those that say that his method of "creative capitalism" is just a method of humanitarian marketing for Microsoft. Others have said that he is not giving away his massive fortune quick enough.

In terms of others' criticism of his later years at Microsoft, perhaps he lost his edge in the competitive world of technology. Or perhaps, as he referenced on his final full day working at Microsoft, he simply changed priorities.

One lesson that we can glean from looking at Gates' life as a whole--and not simply focusing on the fraction of it during which he worked at Microsoft--is that he has always been competitive at what he was passionate about. He no longer prioritizes changing the world of software, but rather has become passionate about changing the world. And that is where his creative, innovative energies have become redirected.

7.4 How to Approach Criticisms of the Competition in Your Life

Competition has been a thread running through Gates' life, including that first family Monopoly game and being prosecuted for monopolistic activities. You may not have the drive (or the billions of dollars) to change world-wide problems, or to revolutionize personal commuting.

However, you can take parts of his approach to his various pursuits, and use them to your advantage. Just as he was resourceful to no end when chasing an objective, take the lessons that you can from this book, and then add all of your intelligence, talent, and resources that are available to chase your own objective.

Published by UNIBOOKS

48220018R00031